CW00694438

EVERY END IS A NEW BEGINNING

To give you courage in times of change

TONI EATTS

Illustrations by Jo Palme

Angus&Robertson

In loving memory of
my father, Noel Eatts,
who taught me life is an adventure.

How to use this book

*T*he most traumatic events I have experienced have been endings – the deaths of my parents, the break-up of major relationships, the break down of significant friendships, the loss of jobs I loved.

As I look back down the road which is my life, these endings stand out like signposts. When I stood at each of those intersections, it felt as if I had come to an extremely painful dead end. But now I am grateful for those events because the road beyond has always turned out to be a new beginning, paved with a deeper understanding of what it is to be human and what an amazing adventure life is.

This book is inspired by the idea that all events are positive. It simply depends on your perspective and your willingness to mourn what needs to be mourned and prepare for the new beginning disguised in every ending.

Use your intuition to guide you to the words that will assist you. Hold thoughts of the ending in your mind, open the book and read whatever your eyes light upon.

This book will:

* comfort you when you can't see the dawn for the dark
* help you to find the courage to cope with change
* help you to find the right words to send to friends and family to celebrate beginnings, such as births, marriages or the start of a new job
* help you to find the right words to comfort friends and relatives who are experiencing a loss
* make the perfect gift for someone you know who is facing changes

The positive statements marked with a can be used as affirmations. Select one which is appropriate and repeat it over and over to yourself each time you feel afraid or negative about the circumstances in which you find yourself.

One of my favourite authors, Stuart Wilde, says that each of us is on our own heroic journey. When you look back over your life you will see that your journey is a series of beginnings and endings separated by periods of peace. Wisdom allows us to approach these changes with inner strength.

If you listen,
You will hear
The silent voice
Of divinity itself.
That you are
Eternal.
That you are
Upon the wheel of Life.
That you were never born
And can never die.

CLEARWATER

Ride those Waves

*I*magine that life is like the ocean. Sometimes it has calm expanses of peace, happiness and rest where you seem to glide across the surface like a swan. Then, suddenly, the surf is up and you have to battle to ride the waves. Or worse – you get dumped by a tidal wave and feel you are drowning.

It is the invisible forces of the moon and wind which haul around these vast oceans of water. It happens silently, constantly. It is the same with our lives. Just when we think we are in control, it can seem as though some silent, unseen hand creates a wave that dumps us, leaving us gasping for breath.

When this happens hold on to the truth that in every end there is a new beginning. And make sure each beginning is a better one!

Ah, my Beloved, fill the Cup that clears
Today of past Regrets and future Fears.

EDWARD FITZGERALD

I cannot help but wonder,
what this time of new beginnings will bring.

PETER LESLIE

I am aware that everyone I meet,
every book I read and every tape
I listen to is my teacher.
I am open and willing to learn
new ways of coping with change.
I attract to myself the information
I need to assist me through this
period of transition and adjustment.

Yesterday
Is the husks that held
The seeds of today.
Take the seeds.
Nurture them.
Let the husks blow away.

CLEARWATER

My Father's Gift

When my father died it felt as if the sun had gone out. Only with his passing did I realise how much I had taken his love for granted.

For the 25 years of my life before he died, he had beamed love to me. His warmth sustained me. He was always there; a psychological underpinning that I only realised existed when I experienced the pain of its loss. But my father's death also gave me a gift.

Like many young people, I had relied on my father financially. I earned my own money but at the very base of me was the unspoken knowledge that if I ever found myself in financial trouble, Dad would bail me out.

When he died, Daddy's little girl was forced to grow up and mature in ways that I wasn't aware of during his life. Even in his death, my father sustained me; helped me to grow with love.

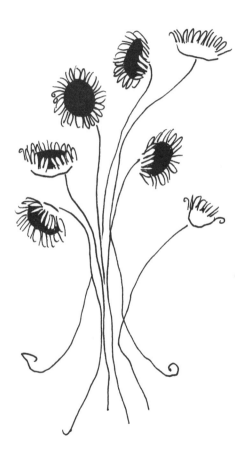

I open my heart
to love
and love flows
easily to me.

I may look back on every sorrow past,
And meet life's peaceful evening with a smile:
As some lone bird, at day's departing hour,
Sings in the sunbeam, of the transient shower
Forgetful, though its wings are wet the while ...

WILLIAM LISLE BOWLES

Is the caterpillar a butterfly in waiting,
or is the butterfly a caterpillar in hiding?

TONI EATTS

When a major love
relationship ends
you are being given another
chance to experience
the joy of falling in love
all over again.

TONI EATTS

Beauty, strength, youth, are flowers but fading seen;
Duty, faith, love, are roots, and ever green.

GEORGE PEELE

passages

A Myth About Marriage

*T*here is a beautiful love story in Greek mythology that gives an insight into the nature of marriage.

Psyche was a mortal, but she was so beautiful that the people in her father's kingdom worshipped her as a goddess. The trouble was, the goddess of femininity, Aphrodite, had a mean and jealous streak. She could not stand the competition so she condemned Psyche to marry Death, the most horrible creature Aphrodite could find. She had Psyche tied to a mountain side and then enlisted the help of her handsome young son, Eros, the god of love. (We also know Eros as Cupid, the one whose job it was to ignite love with his arrows).

Eros had the task of hitting Psyche with one of his arrows so she would fall for the ghastly Death. However, just as he spotted her, he accidentally pricked himself and lost his heart to her. Eros was so besotted he called upon his friend the west wind to waft Psyche down to Paradise Valley, where he married her. You can imagine how Aphrodite reacted when she heard the news!

The story goes on to describe how Psyche and Eros
lived in bliss – the honeymoon phase – for a while, but
then had a major falling out which saw Eros flee.

Psyche pleaded with Aphrodite to reunite them. The
unforgiving Aphrodite set Psyche four impossible tasks
to complete, each of which could lead to her death. It is
the way this myth connects marriage with dying which is
relevant here.

While marriage is a celebration – the beginning of
new life together – it is also an end, a death. This
connection is something we no longer acknowledge
except in the ritual of the "bucks" party or "hens" night.
Superficially, it would seem that men have more to lose
when they marry. Much is made of the man giving up his
bachelor ways. However, in reality, marriage often
enhances a man's life. It can make him emotionally
stronger and give him courage to go out into the world.
It is women who make the greater sacrifice and probably
feel the loss the deepest.

This is the message in this part of the myth. Psyche is
put on the mountain to marry Death. Even though she
ends up with the handsome young Eros, the marriage

still causes some part of her to die. At an unconscious level, many women feel this. They mourn their single status, knowing that they are more emotionally vulnerable as a result of their marriage than their husbands are. If they have children, their dependence on the marriage can increase. The myth alerts us to this part of ourselves. The bride and groom can make allowances for feelings of grief, nostalgia or "cold feet" that one or both might be feeling.

What happened to Psyche? Well, with a little divine help she survived and completed the four tasks set by Aphrodite. The latter was so impressed she relented and granted Psyche immortality so that she and Eros were reunited to live happily ever after.

"Love seeketh not Itself to please,
Nor for itself hath any care;
But for another gives its ease,
And builds a Heaven in Hell's despair."

WILLIAM BLAKE

When I am faced with challenges,
courage comes easily to me.

The
Past,
The
Present
And the
Future
Are
One.
Live in the moment,
My children.
Use the gift of creation
To create paradise.
Know
That humankind
Is but one manifestation
Of the force of life itself.
Know
That all life is connected.

CLEARWATER

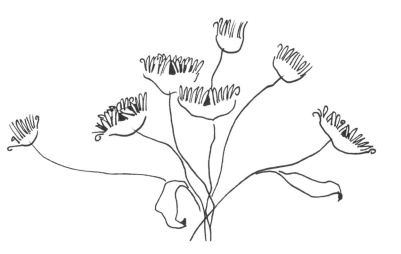

I effortlessly see
all that is positive in any situation.

No more be griev'd at that which thou hast done:
Roses have thorns, and silver fountains mud;
Clouds and eclipses stain both moon and sun,
And loathsome canker lives in sweetest bud.
All men make faults ...

WILLIAM SHAKESPEARE

I am easily able
to achieve all goals I set.
I do this effortlessly,
knowing all the help I need
is there waiting to assist me
when I need it.

Darkness comes,
but it is only passing,
as the light of the soul
can never be overcome.

PETER LESLIE

Allow for Change

At times of great change you may want to end it all.
Many therapists believe that an urge towards
suicide almost always points to the death of an old way
of living or behaving.

If you can kill the right thing – the way of living
which is no longer appropriate – a new phase can grow.
In time, balance is restored, new opportunities open up
and, once again, it feels great to be alive.

All nature is but art, unknown to thee;
All chance, direction, which thou canst not see;
All discord, harmony not understood;
All partial evil, universal good:
And, spite of pride, in erring reason's spite,
One truth is clear: Whatever IS, is RIGHT.

ALEXANDER POPE

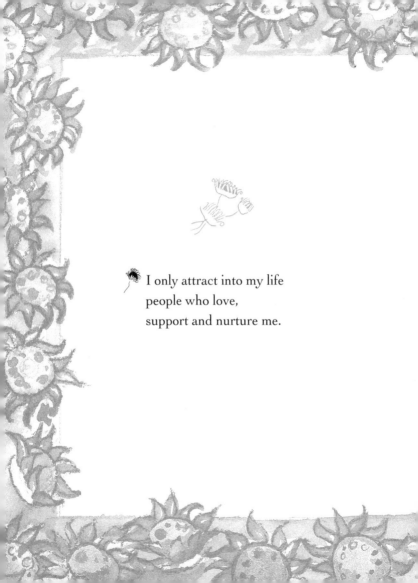

I only attract into my life
people who love,
support and nurture me.

comfort

Transformations

Portion of this yew
Is a man my grandsire knew,
Bosomed here at its foot:
This branch may be his wife,
A ruddy human life
Now turned to a green shoot.

These grasses must be made
Of her who often prayed,
Last century, for repose;
And the fair girl long ago
Whom I often tried to know
May be entering this rose.

So, they are not underground,
But as nerves and veins abound
In the growths of upper air;
And they feel the sun and rain,
And the energy again
That made them what they were!

THOMAS HARDY

You have moved on and I am still here,
learning to accept and love you still.

PETER LESLIE

The King's Ring

There once lived a king who was so wealthy he was able to have the wisest counsellors in all the world living in his kingdom. However, despite all this wisdom being present in his court he was still plagued by terrible bouts of deep depression.

Then one day the king fell in love. He was deliriously happy. He called his wise advisers to him and asked, "How is it that one day I can be so depressed I beg death to come and end my misery. Then, today, I feel so happy and light that I am sure I could fly? I want you to come up with a phrase that applies to both these conditions and gives me hope when I am depressed." The wise men promised they would.

A few days later they returned to the king and presented him with a beautiful golden ring. Inside it was inscribed: "This too shall pass".

Sleep is a reconciling,
A rest that peace begets.
Doth not the sun rise smiling
When fair at even he sets?

ANONYMOUS

I now attract into my life
the perfect partner
for me.

*It was not until the prospect of you leaving my life,
that I realised how strong is my love for you.*

PETER LESLIE

*If your house burns down
it is simply the Universe's way
of telling you to move.*

TONI EATTS

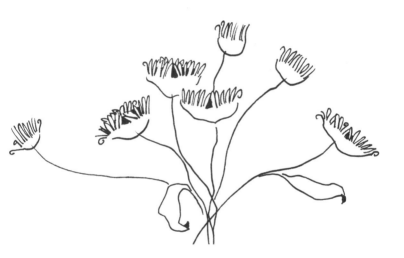

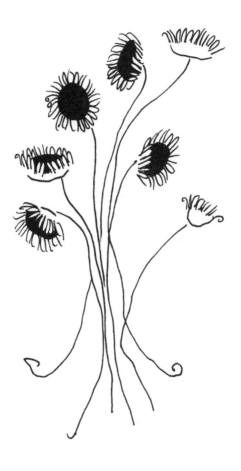

Begin Again

See the sunrise,
A sky of baby hues;
As pink as cheeks to kiss,
As blue as innocent eyes.
The promise of a fresh start.
Gentle awakenings,
First stirrings,
Clouds stretch and yawn
and wisp away.
With hope and joy and love
I begin again today.

TONI EATTS

The Turn

It is not growing like a tree
In bulk doth make man better be;
Or standing long an oak, three hundred year,
To fall a log at last, dry, bald and sere:
A lily of a day
Is fairer far in May;
Although it fall and die that night,
It was the plant and flower of light.
In small proportions we just beauties see,
And in short measures life may perfect be.

BEN JONSON

And to my God my heart did cry
To strengthen me in my distress
And not to leave me succorless.

ANNE BRADSTREET

New Vision

I face the future
with confidence

The Call

With one telephone call
you change my life.
You end endless nights
of takeaway meals for one.
We sit watching the sunrise.
The seagulls call the
last birds of loneliness
from my heart.
I never thought
I'd find you.
But here you are.

TONI EATTS

Dear rose without a thorn,
Thy bud's the babe unborn ...

ROBERT BROWNING

On one who Lived and Died where he was born

When a night in November
Blew forth its bleared airs
An infant descended
His birth-chamber stairs
For the very first time,
At the still, midnight chime;
All unapprehended
His mission, his aim —
Thus, first, one November,
An infant descended
The stairs.

On a night in November
Of weariful cares,
A frail aged figure
Ascended those stairs
For the very last time:
All gone his life's prime,

All vanished his vigour,
And fine, forceful frame:
Thus, last, one November
Ascended that figure
Upstairs.

On those nights in November –
Apart eighty years –
The babe and the bent one
Who traversed those stairs
From the early first time
To the last feeble climb –
That fresh and that spent one –
Were even the same:
Yea, who passed in November
As infant, as bent one,
Those stairs.

Wise child of November!
From birth to blanched hairs,
Descending, ascending,
Wealth-wantless, those stairs;
Who saw quick in time
As a vain pantomime
Life's tending, its ending,
The worth of its fame.
Wise child of November,
Descending, ascending
Those stairs!

THOMAS HARDY

I sleep soundly
knowing my life is growing and unfolding
in the best way possible for me.

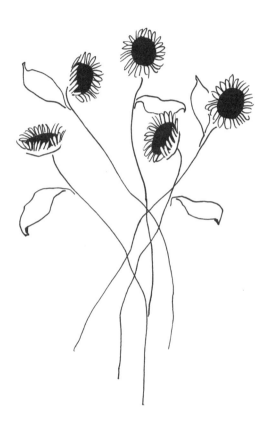

Salute to the Sun

The world awaits its warm embrace
as night flies forth with heavenly grace ...

How privileged am I to witness this birth,
as the light of life moves through its heavenly course.

PETER LESLIE

Recovering From Being Fired

*O*nce I had one of the best jobs I could ever imagine having. I worked with people I truly enjoyed being with, in a job I truly loved and I was well paid. It was a joy to wake up and know I would spend that day at work.

Then came staff changes, imposed on us by management. These resulted in frictions which took the pleasure out of work. Next, the recession kicked in and I was fired, along with dozens of others.

Anyone who has been fired knows how it can damage your self confidence. In my case, I was lucky to have wise and loving friends. One told me to regard this as an opportunity to rethink my working life. He believes that we occasionally give ourselves dramatic kicks in the backside which push us in a new direction that will ultimately be to our benefit. He suggested I look at my work and ask myself, "If I could do anything I liked, what would it be?"

In answering this question, I discovered that I really wanted to be self employed and to work from home. I then began looking at how I could achieve that goal. Some 18 months later I was working from home, earning good money and experiencing less stress. I looked back at the people and circumstances that were the catalyst to my being fired – and blessed them.

If you find yourself in a similar situation, use it to your advantage. Figure out what you really want to do. Seek counselling if you need to. Read books on goal setting and creative visualisation and use these tools to create a positive new life. Go for it!

The bud may have a bitter taste,
But sweet will be the flower.

WILLIAM COWPER

There was a roaring in the wind all night;
The wind came heavily and fell in floods;
But now the sun is rising calm and bright;
The birds are singing in the distant woods ...

WILLIAM WORDSWORTH

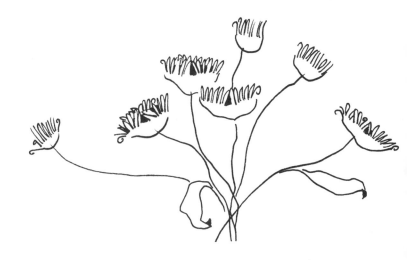

Make the most of being single
because when you are married
you will wish you had.

TONI EATTS

I am open
to new ideas
and new ways of being.

rebuilding

Where There Is Love There Is No Separation

*T*he death of a loved one is the ending that causes the most pain. When my father died there was a tiny part of me which would not accept that I would never see him again. I did not trust that small voice which reassured me that I would reconnect with him some day.

One Easter several years after he died, my mother suddenly became very ill. I flew to my home town to be with her. The nursing staff left us alone. Her breathing was raspy and death seemed near. She was too deeply asleep to notice me. I held her hand and, through my tears, I asked her not to die.

"I'm too young to be an orphan," I said.

Over the next few weeks, my mother's condition improved enough for me to consider returning to Sydney.

Then a colleague telephoned. She had a message from the clairvoyant Margaret Dent, a regular guest on the radio program I produced. Apparently my father had appeared to Margaret to tell me to delay my return, because my mother was deciding whether to pass over or stay on. I had learnt to respect Margaret's ability to communicate with the spirit world, so I put off leaving until my mother's health picked up.

Back in Sydney, Margaret told me Mum had decided to continue living at my request.

"Toni, you told her you were too young to be an orphan," Margaret explained.

I was stunned. I knew that either Margaret could read my mind or that she had received the information from my father, as she claimed. She warned me that my mother only had 12 months.

Forewarned is forearmed. While Mum had no terminal illness, her health never fully recovered. However, she became strong enough for us to take holidays together and connect in a way we never had before. Almost exactly one year later, at around 5 am on Easter Saturday, she passed away relatively peacefully and painlessly.

Some time later, Margaret gave me a private reading and my parents turned up. It was great – just like meeting them for a chat and a cup of tea! Margaret had to act as a spiritual "translator", but she conveyed my Dad's sense of humour and my Mum's sentimental nature so accurately that I was convinced.

This "meeting" did something else for me. It calmed my grief in a way that nothing else could. It is still difficult to explain, but it touched some memory deep within me and awakened a knowing about the continuity of life.

Perhaps it is best expressed in the phrase: "Where there is love there is no separation." From that moment on, I knew this to be true – love never dies. It connects us across time and space and we do meet the people we love again.

But if the while I think on thee, dear friend,
All losses are restored and sorrows end.

WILLIAM SHAKESPEARE

Think then you are TODAY what YESTERDAY
You were - TOMORROW you shall not be less.

EDWARD FITZGERALD

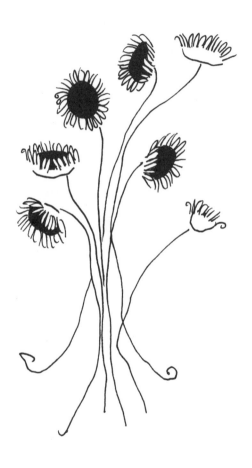

Follow thy fair sun, unhappy shadow;
Though thou be black as night,
And she made all of light,
Yet follow thy fair sun, unhappy shadow.
... Follow still since so thy fates ordained;
The sun must have his shade ...

THOMAS CAMPION

I securely rest in the arms of God
knowing that every happening
is the right happening.

Grow old along with me!
The best is yet to be ...

ROBERT BROWNING

Love After Death

*T*he death of a loved one provides many lessons. It is during times like this that we can draw on the knowledge of people such as clairvoyant Margaret Dent.

Margaret specialises in putting the living in touch with friends and relatives who have died. She says the surviving relatives have the hardest task, because we are the ones who have to stay and complete our different journeys. This can be tough, because we have no memory of why we chose a particular path. Yet however difficult life may seem, it is perfect for our growth.

Another lesson concerns guilt and regret. My mother and I had a troubled relationship.

After she died, Mum said – via Margaret – that she was sorry we had not been closer when she was alive. Margaret says this is common. Most people who have died tell her their greatest regrets are the opportunities they missed to express love to people around them when they were alive.

Death need not mean an end to experiencing that love. We can still share love with the person who has died. The steps are simple.

Firstly work through your grief, then when you are ready, take time out to quiet your mind. Think of the person and tune into the presence of love. It will begin to flow through you as a light, warm energy. You may even see it as a pale pink.

If you have anything you want to say to your loved one, say it. Keep your mind open for a reply. Do not censor what comes next, or think you are making it up. Allow your loved one to talk to you and you might be surprised at what transpires. Even if nothing happens, keep on trying. It can take a little practice because we have to overcome our own in-built cynicism.

Soon after her death, my mother dictated a telegram she wanted sent to honour the wedding of the youngest daughter of her closest friends. It included jokes I was not even privy to. I sent it in her name, as requested. Who was I to argue?

 Every point in my life contains
the potential for a new beginning.
I make the most of these moments
and live my life for my highest good.

Dear Babe, that sleepest cradled by my side,
Whose gentle breathings, heard in this deep calm,
My babe so beautiful! it thrills my heart
With tender gladness, thus to look at thee ...

SAMUEL TAYLOR COLERIDGE

I am now willing
   to release myself from the past
   and to set myself free.

Come, fill the Cup and in the fire of Spring
Your Winter-garment of Repentance fling;
The Bird of Time has but a little way
To flutter – and the Bird is on the Wing.

EDWARD FITZGERALD

I have the power to change my life
by changing my thoughts.
I now choose
to create positive changes in my life
by thinking thoughts of love, peace and joy.

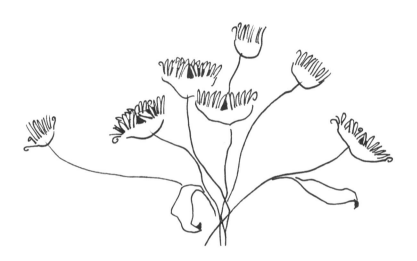

From The Ashes

*A*strology recognises that every end can be turned into a new beginning. Perhaps the most dramatic example is contained in the sign of Scorpio.

Scorpio is often symbolised by the phoenix. According to Greek mythology this colourful bird is about the size of an eagle. When it feels death drawing near, a phoenix builds its own funeral pyre where it sits, singing joyously, until the sun ignites the pyre and the bird burns to ashes. From the ashes crawls a worm, which grows into a new phoenix.

The link with Scorpio is the idea that there needs to be a death before rebirth can occur. This does not mean someone will literally die. The deaths and rebirths are more often in the form of endings and beginnings. If you are born under Scorpio, it is useful to know you could face many endings, all of which contain the possibility for rebirth. The gift contained in Scorpio is the power to regenerate.

The other star signs can take a leaf out of Scorpio's book because everyone faces similar situations at some time during their lives. The phoenix story tells us that, in order for there to be a rebirth, something else will need to be destroyed. It reminds us that we often need to let go completely.

For example, you may not be able to create a new relationship until you have cut all ties with the old one. That's where the fire comes in. The phoenix sings joyfully because it knows that everything will be fine. The fire will burn away all that is old and leave nothing but ashes.

From the ashes crawls a worm – admittedly not a very promising start – and certainly when the fire of change has burnt away our old relationship, or job, or life, we can feel as vulnerable as that worm. Take heart, however. Know that just as the worm will turn into a brand-new, dazzling phoenix, you can regenerate yourself too.

*Ah what adventure,
what new beginnings await.*

PETER LESLIE

Anticipation

Wintertime nighs;
But my bereavement-pain
It cannot bring again:
Twice no one dies.

THOMAS HARDY

Men are disturbed not by things that happen,
but by their opinion of the things that happen.

EPICTETUS

Song from Troilus and Cressida

1

Can life be a blessing,
Or worth the possessing,
Can life be a blessing, if love were away?
Ah, no! though our love all night keep us waking,
And though he torment us with cares all the day,
Yet he sweetens, he sweetens our pains in the taking;
There's an hour at the last, there's an hour to repay.

2

In every possessing
The ravishing blessing,
In every possessing the fruit of our pain,
Poor lovers forget long ages of anguish,
Whate'er they have suffered and done to obtain;
'Tis a pleasure, a pleasure to sigh and to languish,
When we hope, when we hope to be happy again.

JOHN DRYDEN

Retirement Means A New Life

*A*djusting to retirement or to an "empty nest" (if you are a person who has devoted your life to raising children) is a challenge.

Mostly, our sense of self is tied up with what we do, not with who we truly are. Work or family give our lives meaning and, when this focus is removed, we can feel worthless.

If one partner is experiencing this passage, it can rock the relationship. The person looking on can either feel helpless or become overly enthusiastic in suggesting new pastimes.

Counsellors recognise that grief is a natural response to a major life change; they also advise that it is a process that takes time. Some people simply take longer to adjust than others.

Do your grieving – then try to see the glass as being half full, rather than half empty. You are more than just the job you held or the family you nurtured. You are a unique human being, with talents and interests still to be developed. Now that you have fewer responsibilities you can indulge yourself.

Make a list of the things you have always wanted to do. Then, set about doing them.

If you need inspiration, think of Betty Lister-Davis. After decades of raising a family and working as a nurse, Betty – aged 51 – studied for an undergraduate degree in psychology and then a masters degree in counselling. She then put this knowledge to good use by working in major public hospitals, where she counselled the staff.

Now 71 years old, Betty is carving a new career for herself as an actress, taking short parts in various television series and commercials. In the past few years she has also been ballooning and canoeing, and she has taken ballroom dancing lessons.

Betty says you have to have a dream. "Expect good things to happen and, if you think long and strong enough, they will," she says.

If Betty's story is not enough inspiration for you, remember that many great artists and writers did not flower until their later years. Also, the younger generation needs people with your experience of life and special talents to help light their way.

Live each day as it comes and make the most of every one.

Our God, our help in ages past,
Our hope for years to come,
Be thou our guard while troubles last,
And our eternal home.

ISAAC WATTS

Proud Songsters

The thrushes sing as the sun is going,
And the finches whistle in ones and pairs,
And as it gets dark loud nightingales
In bushes
Pipe, as they can when April wears,
As if all Time were theirs.

These are brand new birds of twelve-months' growing,
Which a year ago, or less than twain,
No finches were, nor nightingales,
Nor thrushes,
But only particles of grain,
And earth, and air, and rain.

THOMAS HARDY

Grief melts away
Like snow in May,
As if there were no such cold thing.

GEORGE HERBERT

Life carries forward, the past is framed,
framed in memories of love and laughter.

PETER LESLIE

You will decide on a matter
and it will be established for you
and light will shine on your ways.

JOB 22:28

Wheel of Fortune

*O*ne of the major cards in the tarot deck is the Wheel
of Fortune. It symbolises the changing external
events in our lives.

Imagine a wheel. The hub is your true self. It does
not move but it causes the outer rim to revolve. This
symbolises the connection between your spirit (your true
self) and your fate (the events in your life).

Now, imagine the wheel moving clockwise. You are at
the top, enjoying the rich rewards of life. As the wheel
turns that good fortune diminishes until you slide right
under the wheel. Here it feels as if you are being
squashed by events, literally run over by life. Then
imagine the wheel continuing to turn, propelling you up
and out from under the wheel. Life becomes more
comfortable as you once again head towards success.

During all this your true spirit sits at the centre,
untouched. It calmly observes the events and the tests
that fate unfolds for you knowing that, no matter what

happens, the wheel will continue to turn. The more you listen to this true self, the more power you can consciously exercise over your destiny.

We often perceive events as being either "good" or "bad". Thinking of the Wheel of Fortune shows us how a greater force can be behind what seem to be random changes in our lives.

Balance

I instinctively know
when it is the time for waiting
and when it is the time for action.

All nature seems at work. Slugs leave their lair –
The bees are stirring – birds are on the wind –
And Winter slumbering in the open air
Wears on his smiling face a dream of Spring!

SAMUEL TAYLOR COLERIDGE

Remember not that which is lost,
remember that which we gained in friendship and love.

PETER LESLIE

Heredity

I am the family face;
Flesh perishes, I live on,
Projecting trait and trace
Through time to times anon,
And leaping from place to place
Over oblivion.

The years-heired feature that can
In curve and voice and eye
Despise the human span
Of durance – that is I;
The eternal thing in man,
That heeds no call to die.

THOMAS HARDY

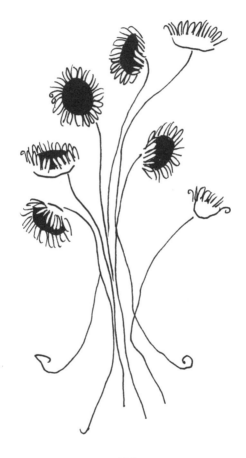

I am open and willing to learn.
I find peace
even in the toughest lessons.

I was entangled in the world of strife,
Before I had the power to change my life.

GEORGE HERBERT

I expect the most wonderful things
to happen right now –
and they do!

Mother Love

Small angel,
gentle cherub.
You come as a stranger
who knows the secrets
of my womb.
Your birth marks the beginning,
of a new me.
Never again can I think of myself
as a woman alone.
Labour's strenuous passage
initiated me into the
eternal mysteries of mother love.
I gaze into your ageless eyes
and see wisdom, love, promise.
All new
All reward
All I need.

TONI EATTS

What though the radiance which was once so bright
Be now forever taken from my sight,
Though nothing can bring back the hour
Of splendour in the grass, of glory in the flower;
We will grieve not, rather find
Strength in what remains behind;
In the primal sympathy
Which having been must ever be;
In the soothing thoughts that spring
Out of human suffering;
In the faith that looks through death,
In years that bring the philosophic mind.

WILLIAM WORDSWORTH

To every thing there is a season,
and a time to every purpose
under the heaven ...

ECCLESIASTES 3:1

Shrug off the restraints
That you have allowed others
To place upon you.
You are limitless.
There is nothing you cannot
Achieve.
There is no sadness in life
That cannot be reversed.
There is no sickness
That cannot be cured.
Each second
You can be reborn.
Each second
There can be
A new beginning.
It is choice.
It is your choice.

CLEARWATER

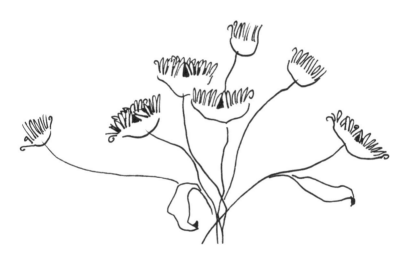

What if we still ride on, we two
With life forever old yet new,
Changed not in kind but in degree,
The instant made eternity –
And heaven just prove that I and she
Ride, ride together, forever ride?

ROBERT BROWNING

acceptance

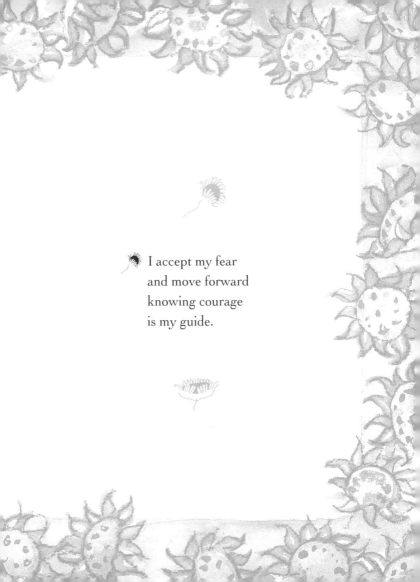

I accept my fear
and move forward
knowing courage
is my guide.

And see the rivers, how they run
Through woods and meads, in shade and sun;
Sometimes swift, sometimes slow,
Wave succeeding wave, they go
A various journey to the deep,
Like human life to endless sleep!

JOHN DYER

God's in his heaven –
All's right with the world!

ROBERT BROWNING

I move forward knowing
this is the right path for me.

How happy and joyous am I to see you reborn,
renewed and forever changing and growing.

PETER LESLIE

Consequences Of Suicide

When someone dies, the person who loved them most may feel an urge to kill themselves too, rather than live alone.

However, according to those with expertise in spiritual matters, suicide has negative consequences. They say life is a gift and that it is a privilege to have the opportunity to live and grow on this physical plane because of the particular lessons offered.

If you opt out of your lessons, this choice has an effect on your future growth and on the people around you.

In the spirit realm you will be gently made aware of these consequences. You might be surprised by the number of people affected by your death. These could range from those closest to you to people you had never considered – for example, work colleagues, the greengrocer you chat to, or your neighbours. In death you will become aware of the pain you have caused.

Realise that the pain you feel now will pass. What seems like a bleak ending will blossom into better times.

If you have had someone close to you commit suicide, you will be familiar with the sense of guilt it can impose on those left behind. You ask yourself questions, such as "Why didn't I stop it?" Or if it was a close relative you may worry that you could be prone to suicide too, or that it is a family tendency you might pass on to your children.

If you are the one left behind you can ease this guilt by realising that we are all ultimately responsible for our own actions. The person who killed themselves is responsible for that action, not you.

Work through your grief. Then try to forgive the person who died. With forgiveness comes a particular energy – it gives the person who took their life strength and courage and this, in turn, flows back to you.

How should I praise thee, Lord!
...Whether I fly with angels, fall with dust,
Thy hands made both, and I am there.
Thy power and love, my love and trust,
Make one place everywhere.

GEORGE HERBERT

I allow my life to unfold,
trusting that all events
are for my highest good.

A Contemplation upon Flowers

Brave flowers, that I could gallant it like you,
And be as little vain;
You come abroad and make a harmless show,
And to your beds of earth again;
You are not proud, you know your birth,
For your embroidered garments are from earth.

You do obey your months and times, but I
Would have it ever spring;
My fate would know no winter, never die,
Nor think of such a thing;
Oh that I could my bed of earth but view,
And smile and look as cheerfully as you.

Oh teach me to see death and not to fear,
But rather to take truce;
How often have I seen you at a bier,
And there look fresh and spruce;
You fragrant flowers then teach me that my breath
Like yours may sweeten and perfume my death.

HENRY KING

Grow Old Together

I want us to grow old together,
we two.
Today you stand before me
pledging your love.
A few yesterdays ago
it was dinner you offered
and my heart you took home.
Some people love easily.
Effortlessly.
They love as easily as you laugh.
It is rare for me.
My heart is a cautious thing.

Today you stand before me
pledging your love.
I have never before known
such joy.
Such sweet surrender.
Of your love, I have no doubt.

Couple it with commitment
and I will be forever yours.
Because
I want us to grow old together;
we two.

TONI EATTS

Go, birds of spring: let winter have his fee;
Let a bleak paleness chalk the door,
So all within be livelier than before.

GEORGE HERBERT

Many of you
Have seen tears
And disappointments.
You regret that which was.
You gaze upon your mistakes
And you carry your guilt.
But
Were they mistakes?
Or
Did you make them
That you might learn?

CLEARWATER

See how on every bough the birds express
In their sweet notes their happiness
They all enjoy and nothing spare;
But on their mother nature lay their care ...

JOHN DRYDEN

I trust that
whatever I need to know
will be revealed to me
in the most appropriate manner
at the most appropriate time.

Relieving The Trauma

*I*n the movie, *An Unmarried Woman*, Jill Clayburgh plays the lead character, a happily married woman. Then her husband tells her he wants a divorce so he can marry someone younger. The shock is so great that she vomits in the street.

Any major stress has an impact on your physical and emotional wellbeing. You can feel as though you are riding a rollercoaster of emotional responses, such as:

* shock – disbelief at what has happened
* fear – panic over what people might think
* anger – feelings of rage and "Why me?"
* numbness – not feeling anything at all or experiencing lethargy
* guilt – worrying that you have not said or done the appropriate thing
* sadness – feelings of loss

Emotional injury is often harder to see than physical injury, but it is no less real. Symptoms might include:

* eating more or less than usual

❊ increasing your alcohol or drug intake

❊ difficulty with sleeping

❊ mood swings

❊ outbursts of anger

❊ reliving your feelings at the time of the trauma

❊ feeling jumpy

❊ trouble concentrating

❊ headaches, tense muscles or heart palpitations.

If you recognise yourself here, try these suggestions to ease your distress:

❊ be kind to yourself

❊ avoid sugary or junk food and caffeine

❊ take a stress reduction vitamin supplement

❊ resist the urge to try and escape from your feelings through drugs and alcohol

❊ take regular relaxing baths, adding the essential oils of lavender and sandalwood to soothe you; go swimming if you can

❊ seek the company of supportive people who allow you to talk, or not to talk, as you wish

❊ see a counsellor to "debrief". Often it is difficult to

tell friends and family all you feel because you want to spare their feelings. A counsellor can allow you to say it all. Try it. You will feel better.

Though I fail, I weep:
Though I halt in pace,
Yet I creep
To the throne of grace.

GEORGE HERBERT

As, when a tree's cut down, the secret root
Lives underground, and thence new branches shoot ...

JOHN DRYDEN

Each Age Has Its Glory

I see an elderly man
sunning himself in the park.
Skin as thin as rice paper.
Hair as fine as feathers on
a freshly hatched chick.

I wonder how he has coped
with life's bitter twists
and devastating turns.

Each age has its glory.

A toddler's tentative steps.
A teenager's carelessness.
The world-is-my-oyster twenties.
Those levelling middle years
when you realise God is an
accountant.